IMAGES
of America

DOYLESTOWN

Dedication

To the memory of W.W.H. Davis (1820–1910),
statesman, lawyer, soldier, publisher, writer,
and historian of Doylestown.

IMAGES
of America

DOYLESTOWN

The County Seat of Bucks County, Pennsylvania

Ed Ludwig, Brooks McNamara, and Betty Strecker
for the
Doylestown Historical Society

ARCADIA
PUBLISHING

Published by Arcadia Publishing
Charleston, South Carolina

Library of Congress Catalog Card Number: 00-107746

For all general information contact Arcadia Publishing at:
Telephone 843-853-2070
Fax 843-853-0044
E-mail sales@arcadiapublishing.com
For customer service and orders:
Toll-Free 1-888-313-2665

Visit us on the Internet at www.arcadiapublishing.com

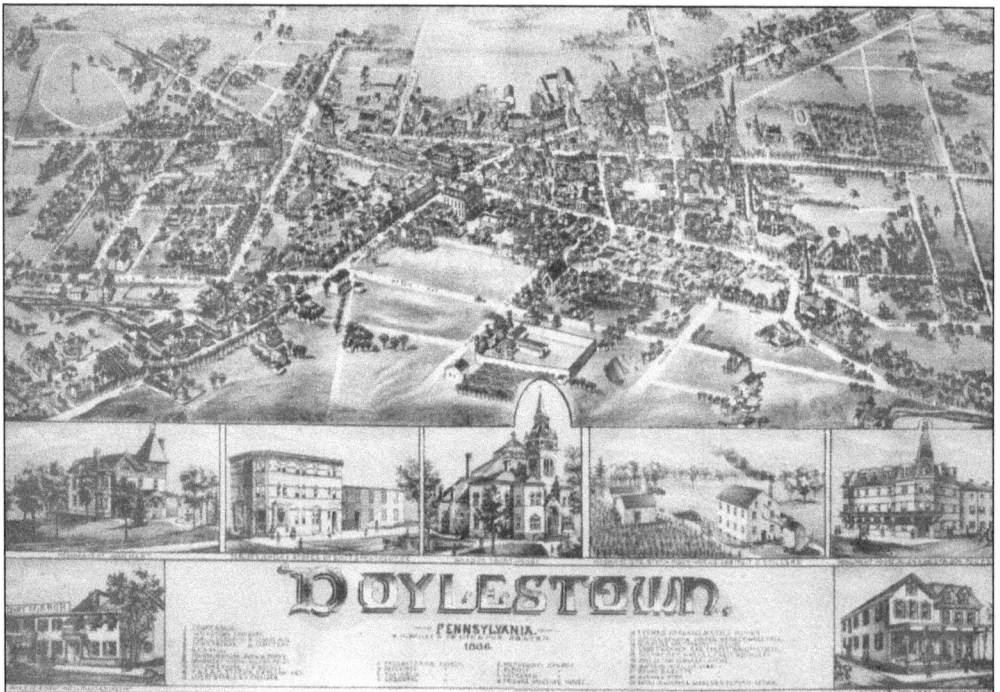

This map of Doylestown was published in 1886 by S.H. Bailey & Company of Boston. Clockwise, from the lower left, are insets of the Bucks County Mirror building, the John Hart Residence, Seigler's Jewelry Store, the Bucks County Court House, Heist's Steam Cider Works and Fruit Distillery, the Monument House, and the Kramer General Store. (Map courtesy of Spruance Library, Bucks County Historical Society, published by the Doylestown Community Association in 1982 to commemorate the 300th anniversary of Bucks County.)

CONTENTS

ACKNOWLEDGMENTS

This books represents the work of many people. The Doylestown Historical Society thanks the committee that prepared the book: Ed Ludwig, president; Betty Strecker, first vice president; and Brooks McNamara, director. The committee gathered the illustrations, and Brooks organized the chapters and wrote the text, with editorial and graphics support. Access to most of the photographs resulted from a front-page article on the project written by Ed Levenson, a reporter for the *Intelligencer*, Doylestown's daily newspaper. Particular thanks are due Jack Regenhard (author of Arcadia's *Hatboro*) and Syd and Sharon Martin, who cheerfully opened their magnificent collections to the society. Their contributions, together with a substantial number from Betty Strecker, make up the major portion of the images in this book.

Others who generously contributed photographs are Eddy Blain, Glen Cooper, Kay Ewing, Florence Histand, Mary Howe, Joan Jarrett, Bill Neis, Bryan Oliver, and Harry and Alice Sammler. Those who submitted pictures that were not used are not mentioned by name but are much thanked. Our friend and towering relative, the Bucks County Historical Society, through its Spruance Library and top-notch librarian, Betsy Smith, and the James A. Michener Art Museum also made their archives available to us. Bill Neis, our mayor, gave us special assistance in authenticating the 1898 photograph of the first trolley car in Doylestown; he also found out the exact date it was taken. Barker Gummere, coauthor of *Trolley Cars of Bucks County, Pennsylvania*, kindly let us use his print of the cover photograph. Peter Turco, our editor at Arcadia Publishing, was invariably helpful and patient. Directors Barbara Dommel, George Bush, Jon McSurdy, Nick Molloy, and Herman Silverman played significant roles. Jon drove the book's images to Dover, New Hampshire, and waited two days for them to be scanned, so as to minimize the risk of loss for the contributors of the originals. Jean Pennie is thanked for her proficient word processing and Vicki Azar for her work in final assembly of the draft. A considerable effort was made to ensure the accuracy of the written material. We would welcome being informed of any mistakes.

Only institutional credits have been noted with the individual photographs.

INTRODUCTION

DOYLESTOWN THROUGH THE YEARS

The area in which Doylestown now rests was originally part of a tract given by William Penn to the "Free Society of Traders" in 1682. This land contained some 20,000 acres, about 8,600 of which were in the adjoining communities of Warwick, New Britain, and Hilltown. In the early 18th century, the 2,000 or so remaining acres (on both sides of the present Court Street in Doylestown) were purchased by Jeremiah Langhorne. In 1745, William Doyle asked the authorities for what is today called a liquor license for an inn near the site of the present Lenape Hall. Doylestown, a crossroads, had come into being, although its name as one word did not appear in print until 1778, having previously been referred to as "Doyle's town" or "Doyle Town."

During the Revolution, the area was an outpost of the American army, under the command of Gen. James Lacey, but no battles took place here. It is documented that on the stormy night of June 20, 1778, Commander in Chief George Washington stayed in Doylestown on his way to Valley Forge, some 20 miles to the southeast. Indeed, Doylestown was isolated throughout the 18th century. Not a great deal of significance happened, though early in the 19th century two events occurred that would help to shape the town's future. The Reverend Uriah Dubois arrived and founded the Union Academy in 1805, which also housed Dubois's embryonic Presbyterian Church. About the same time, there was the appearance of a newspaper, the *Pennsylvania Correspondent*. Another occurrence, in the first years of the 19th century, would be perhaps of even greater importance to the borough; in 1810, Doylestown became the county seat of Bucks County, and in 1812, the first Bucks County Court House was dedicated in Doylestown. It was incorporated as a borough in 1838, and adjoining the borough is a separate municipality, Doylestown Township. Most notable over the years has been the huge number of old structures that continue to exist in downtown Doylestown and nearby.

At the end of the 1920s, however, Doylestown was still a sleepy town, largely unknown to most outsiders. Its claims to notoriety were modest. It had been the once-supposed birthplace of Daniel Boone and was the girlhood home of Margaret Mead. It served as a visual subject for many of the Bucks County School of artists. It was the town where the not-yet-famous James Michener grew up in abject poverty and where seed magnate W. Atlee Burpee had developed his internationally known Fordhook Farm, the site of the Burpee Seed Company. And, of course, there were the great—many thought eccentric—architectural creations of

Henry Mercer: two castles (Fonthill and the Mercer Museum) less than a mile apart from each other. Because it was a particularly handsome area, Doylestown had once been a tourist center, especially for residents of Philadelphia, but tourist activities were in decline.

Then, beginning around 1930, central Bucks County—and with it the Doylestown area—was "discovered" by New Yorkers and Philadelphians, many in the arts, drawn by the seemingly endless supply of beautiful, cheap land, old fieldstone houses, Pennsylvania Dutch folklore and inexpensive antiques. Among those who bought or rented places in Doylestown or in the nearby area were Oscar Hammerstein, George Kaufman, Moss Hart, Charles Sheeler, Pearl Buck, S.J. Pearlman, and Budd Shulberg, as well as a number of movie and other theatrical personalities. The town was to become the boyhood home of Stephen Sondheim.

Starting in the 1950s, Bucks County soon became the fastest growing county in the state, doubling in population—to 300,000 by 1960 and to 600,000 in 2000. While most of the growth was in the lower part of the county, the effects on Doylestown Borough as the county seat, located in the center of the county, were significant. Population and traffic increased dramatically, and the borough is now surrounded by housing developments, shopping centers, and commercial strips. Still, the integrity of the downtown has been maintained and revitalized. With its burst of new and trendy restaurants, its architecture, museums, and authenticity, it has become again a visitors' destination, one of the most popular in the Philadelphia metropolitan area.

This book is made up of historic photographs, postcards, and other items from private collections, mostly from the 19th century up to about World War II. In addition, however, it reflects some of the history of a prosperous and unusually beautiful area that, over the years, has attracted vacationers, artists, celebrities, and historians—and many enthusiastic permanent residents. They came to the borough—a community that is truly unusual—from many directions. Doylestown's residents take great pride in the knowledge that so much of its history has survived and can be witnessed and enjoyed today. Come visit Doylestown if you have not already been here, and you will be sure to agree.

"Such, in a few words," as Davis put it at the end of his charming book *Doylestown, Old and New* (1904), "is our summing up of the present and prospective Doylestown, whose modest history we have attempted to portray."

One

PUBLIC SPACES

Doylestown has always been proud of its public buildings, many of which have survived to the present day. One of the most impressive, now gone, was the so-called new Bucks County Court House, built in 1878. It replaced a smaller structure that was no longer adequate and, in turn, was replaced by the present building in 1960. This section offers a selection of photographs and other items related to Doylestown's public spaces, both those that survive (a surprising number) and those that are no longer in existence.

Here is the original Bucks County Court House. Note the date of the building's construction on the pediment. The men shown on the porch are presumably lawyers and perhaps judges. The Bucks County Bar Association, organized in 1873, now has about 650 members. (Note: Until the 1950s, "courthouse" was two words. The first two courthouses—1812 and 1878—are referred to as such in this book.)

11

The 1878 Bucks County Court House is decorated for the Old Home Week Centennial Celebration of 1912, honoring the first courthouse, opened in 1812. In the 20th century, the building became too small and cramped for the activities of the court and for the administration of the county. It was torn down and replaced with a larger structure in 1960.

This is the main courtroom of the 1878 Bucks County Court House—pie-shaped, with two large fireplaces. Portraits of judges who served there line the walls. A radiator for the new device of central heating stood in the middle of the room.

The "new" or third Bucks County Court House is located, like its predecessors, near Monument Square, at the top of the Main Street hill. The 1868 monument to the men of the 104th Regiment of Pennsylvania Volunteers is in the foreground, and Court Street is in the background.

This is a closer view of the Civil War Monument. Several of the old buildings have been razed over the years.

The entrance to the Bucks County Prison, shown in 1884 and located on Pine Street, became known locally as the "Pine Street Hotel" during the benign stewardship of Warden John D. Case (1962–1978). Much of the structure is now remodeled as part of the James A. Michener Art Museum, where there is a fine collection of the work of Bucks County and other artists.

14

Shown is the sally port and yard of the "Pine Street Hotel." The space now serves as a sculpture garden, open both to the James A. Michener Art Museum and the county library next-door.

Transition, by the noted sculptor Raymond Barger, was erected in the yard of the former Bucks County Prison when it became part of the James A. Michener Art Museum in 1988. Shown behind it is a former cell block that has been given a new facade.

The second Doylestown Hospital, opened in 1939, was located on Belmont Avenue and is now a nursing home. There have been three hospitals in Doylestown, all owned by the Village Improvement Association (VIA). The first, on Oakland and Pine (1923), was outgrown. The present hospital (1975) is located near the edge of the borough in Doylestown Township.

The Centennial Fountain once stood in the park near the 1878 Bucks County Court House, close to the Court Street entrance. Two of the old houses, now law offices, are shown in the background.

16

This flagstaff was once seen in the courthouse park. It was said to have been the tallest flagpole in the United States, with a height of 176 feet.

The Doylestown National Bank and Trust Company was located near the courthouse on Monument Square. Both the building and the bank no longer survive. The tower of the courthouse is seen in the background.

The former Melinda Cox Free Library, originally a bank building, was a gift of a citizen of Doylestown whose house still stands on State Street. The library has been moved to a site next to the James A. Michener Art Museum. The old structure is now used by the Bucks County controller. In the photograph, it is decorated for the Old Home Week Centennial Celebration of 1912.

This is the Masonic Temple, originally known as Beneficial Hall, of Doylestown's Masonic Order, Lodge No. 245, Free and Accepted Masons, shown during its 150th anniversary celebration. It is one of the oldest public buildings on East State Street. During the 19th century, it was the temporary location of several churches, among them St. Paul's Episcopal Church.

Jan.	17	July	17
Feb.	21	Aug.	21
Mar.	20	Sept.	18
April	17	Oct.	16
May	15	Nov.	20
June	19	Dec.	18

Masonic Register

DOYLESTOWN

R.A.C.
NO. 270.

1952

Shown is one side of a wallet card that contains a listing of the officers of various groups using the Masonic structure, as well as meeting times for 1952. Information about one group—the Mizpah Commandery, No. 96, K.T.—appears in the illustration.

Members of the Bucks County Bar Association, 1902, pose on the steps of the second Bucks County Court House. The modern home of the bar association is located at the corner of State and Church Streets, where Dr. Hayman's hospital once stood.

The present Doylestown Hospital was built in 1975 and has had three additions. It has a 180-bed capacity. Its owner, the Village Improvement Association, is comprised of women volunteers and was founded in 1895. The VIA's contributions to Doylestown have been exceptional.

Of the many concession stands that have been at the Doylestown Fair, this one is probably from the early 1900s. The fairgrounds also contained a popular racetrack, originally used for trotting and, later, for auto races.

20

The Doylestown Annual Fair was held at the fairgrounds on East Court Street across from Fonthill, the castlelike concrete and tile mansion built by Henry Mercer. The picture was taken September 12, 1937, from the top of a 130-foot ladder, as Ferris wheels, swings, and sideshows were being unloaded. (From Spruance Library, Bucks County Historical Society.)

The Almshouse, or the Bucks County "Poor House" (now the Neshaminy Manor), is a few miles south of Doylestown and was dedicated on May 4, 1809. The building is used by the county for administrative offices. James Michener described his boyhood days there in his second novel *The Fires of Spring* (1949).

21

The Borough Dam, or reservoir, used to be a source of water for the borough. In 1995, the pond, in bad repair, was rebuilt under the leadership of Michael Stachel in an enormous all-volunteer effort. For many years, it has been used for an annual fishing project for youngsters and is always packed on the opening day of trout season in April. At present, the program called Friends of the Borough Dam is primarily supported by the Doylestown Rotary Club and Trout Unlimited.

The County Theater, an Art Deco classic, was constructed in the 1930s. In 1993, after many years of financial difficulty, it was purchased by a community group led by John Toner and rehabilitated through a large fundraising effort. With its first-run, top-quality films, it has become an important part of the downtown. A few years ago, AT&T used a picture of the theater in a magazine advertisement.

Two

HISTORIC HOUSES OF
WORSHIP AND SCHOOLS

The original Presbyterian Church was founded in a room in the Union Academy by the Reverend Uriah Dubois. Its first building was constructed in 1815. Perhaps the first surviving public structure of importance was its second home, built on East Court Street in 1870–1871 on the site of the original church. The chancel is 90 feet long and 60 feet wide and seats some 650 people. The walls are between 2 and 2.5 feet thick. Doylestown is—and was—the home of a number of historic structures. Several, like the Methodist Episcopal Church (1838), have been converted to other uses. For example, that church became Borough Hall, which houses the meeting place and administrative offices of the Doylestown Borough Council. But a number of early houses of worship survive in or near Doylestown, including the First Presbyterian Church (1815); the Doylestown Friends Meeting (present building 1836), St. Paul's Episcopal Church (1848), the Salem United Church of Christ (1897), and the Mennonite Church (1900). In 1959, Temple Judea, the first Reform Synagogue in Bucks County, was organized in Doylestown and used the Friends Meeting House until it built its own structure in 1967 on Swamp Road. Its present congregation consists of about 250 families.

Doylestown and the surrounding area have also been home to many public and private schools, including the long-vanished Union Academy on East Court Street; two virtually forgotten private schools (for girls, the Linden Academy, and for boys, the Doylestown English and Classical Seminary); a parochial school, St. Bernard's School (later Our Lady of Mount Carmel School); the Doylestown Borough School, destroyed by fire (1973); Linden Elementary School; Doyle Elementary School; Lenape Junior High School; Central Bucks West High School; and Delaware Valley College, formerly the National Farm School.

The First Presbyterian Church of Doylestown, still in active use on East Court Street, is probably the oldest house of worship in Doylestown. It is the second church structure to exist on the site. Construction of the church building was begun in 1815. Its founder, the Reverend Uriah Dubois, is buried in the churchyard.

St. Mary's Roman Catholic Church and the parish house were located on State Street. Both are now gone. A new church has replaced the old one at approximately the same location.

24

The old First Baptist Church was completed in 1876. The structure became inadequate for the congregation, which built a new church on West State Street. The building and the former parsonage next-door were remodeled as offices, now called the Landmark Building.

Methodist Church, Doylestown, Pa.

Like the Baptists, the Methodists of Doylestown found their church building—at Main Street and Taylor Alley—inadequate and built a new church on the edge of Doylestown. The old structure still stands and is now the home of several Baptist congregations.

St. Paul's (formerly All Saints') Episcopal Church faces Oakland at Pine Streets, 1848. The church, which was once featured on a *Saturday Evening Post* cover, survives. The house at left was replaced by an addition to the church.

Shown are the Salem United Church of Christ and its manse on East Court Street. The church, dedicated in 1897, originally served Doylestown's German community. The late-Victorian manse was torn down (1982), but the church survives and contains a collection of tiles, gift of Henry Mercer.

The Friends Meeting House, on Oakland Avenue, was built in 1836. Bucks County (and Doylestown) has a large Quaker population, which helps to explain the presence in the borough of a station of the Underground Railroad before the Civil War.

The modern National Shrine of Our Lady of Czestochowa, near Doylestown, was built in the 1950s as a refuge from then Communist-dominated Poland. The shrine is seen from the east in this view.

Miss George Watson

To LINDEN FEMALE SEMINARY, Dr.

For the Term Ending *March 17th* 1880.

To Board, Washing, Fuel, and Light, $	To Drawing,	
" Tuition,	12.00	" Oil Painting,
" Instrumental Music,		" French,
" Use of Instrument,		" Books,
" Vocal Music,		" Rent of Books, .50

$12.50

Received Payment,

McGinty, Cheap Job Printer, Helst's Hall, Doylestown, Pa.

This bill, dated 1880, is from the Linden Female Seminary. The seminary was on East Street and Maple Avenue, on the present site of a nursing home. Henry Mercer rented the building and used it as a temporary residence during the building of Fonthill on nearby East Court Street.

This print depicts the private boys' school, the English and Classical Seminary, on West Street. The structure became a summer hotel, the Oakland, about the turn of the 19th century and was later demolished.

The Doylestown public grade school (left) and high school once stood at the corner of East Court and Broad Streets on the former site of the Union Academy that had been attended by W.W.H. Davis in the 1830s. The anthropologist Margaret Mead and the writer James Michener graduated from Doylestown High School in 1918 and 1925, respectively. The buildings burned to the ground in 1973, and the site is now a parking lot for the Bucks County Courthouse and Administration Building.

The Doylestown High School band of 1928 is assembled in front of the school building on East Court Street.

National Farm School, Doylestown, Pa.

This was the main building of the National Farm School, now known as Delaware Valley College. The school was originally formed at the turn of the century to interest young Jewish men in "the love of the land" and to teach them agriculture. It became a nonsectarian liberal arts college.

Three

THE MERCERS AND
THEIR LEGACY

Henry Mercer had an influence on Doylestown far beyond his impact as a wealthy and powerful citizen. Mercer's relatives—both Chapmans and Mercers—were also influential in the Doylestown area, and they left him financially independent. Born on June 24, 1856, privately educated, and a Harvard graduate, he studied law at the University of Pennsylvania but did not become a practicing lawyer. Instead, he expressed an early and compelling interest in anthropology and archeology; toward the end of the century, he became heavily involved in the still youthful Bucks County Historical Society. He also developed a new type of collection, what he called "The Tools of the Nation Maker," which linked together Old World origins and American innovations.

In 1880, W.W.H. Davis had founded the Bucks County Historical Society, with headquarters in Doylestown, where it remains. Mercer's prodigious contributions included his tool collection and their repository, the society's main building, the Mercer Museum. Eventually, Mercer's famous architectural endeavors with concrete took place. They included his home Fonthill (1910), his Moravian Pottery and Tile Works (1912), and the Mercer Museum (1916). His structures, like his tool collection, were new departures for their day. About the use of concrete at Fonthill, he once said, "We proposed not to copy stone, or wood, or metal, or anything else but . . . we intended to let the cement stand upon its own merit, casting itself into any reasonable shape, by and for its own law."

Mercer died in 1930, having been a leader of the Bucks County Historical Society for many years. He is buried in the churchyard of the Doylestown Presbyterian Church.

Henry Mercer was undoubtedly an unusual and sometimes difficult person, but his interests were broad, his talents remarkable, and his contributions to Doylestown—and to the history of America—were considerable. Here he is shown in the prime of life with one of his many beloved dogs.

The Village Improvement Association's headquarters are located in the historic James-Lorah House, on North Main Street. The house, the birthplace of Henry Mercer, was left to the VIA and contains, as well as a collection of interesting antiques, an auditorium for the VIA and other community activities.

Frosterly was the home of Fanny Chapman (1846–1924), Henry Mercer's aunt. The house was built in 1871 by Henry's grandfather on a farm he owned near Doylestown. It was later demolished.

In 1927, this pool was given to Doylestown Borough in honor of the memory of Fanny Chapman by her nephew, William Mercer. The pool continues to be operated by the borough. Since its inception, it has offered swimming lessons for the community's youngsters, as well as lifesaving and other adult programs. In 1975, two pools were added. (From Spruance Library, Bucks County Historical Society.)

This is the main facade of Mercer's estate Fonthill (1910), on East Court Street in Doylestown, one of Mercer's engineering feats in concrete. He chose concrete because it was easily molded, low cost, fireproof, and worked well with tiles, which he collected internationally and eventually had manufactured in his own Moravian Pottery and Tile Company, located on the same tract as Fonthill.

Fonthill is shown from the southwest. The estate, now managed by the Bucks County Historical Society, is open to the public.

The dining room at Fonthill was used extensively by Mercer for entertaining guests.

The Yellow Room at Fonthill was one of a number of guest bedrooms. The concrete tile–topped dresser, the built-in wooden closets, and the bureau were all designed by Mercer.

An exterior view of Mercer's Moravian Pottery and Tile Works dates from not long after its construction in 1912.

Shown is a detail of Mercer's Tile Works. The structure, which still exists, is located on the same tract as Fonthill.

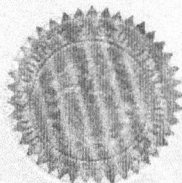

This is to Certify

That *John C. Swartley* of *Doylestown* having been duly elected a n *active* Member of the

BUCKS COUNTY HISTORICAL SOCIETY,

Founded 1880.

Incorporated 1885.

in accordance with the provisions of the Charter and By-Laws, the *ninth* day of *August* A. D. *1898*, he is entitled to all the privileges of such membership.

In Testimony Whereof, the Officers have hereunto affixed their signatures, and the seal of said Society, at Doylestown, Pa., this *Eighteenth* day of *January* A. D. *1899*

W. W. H. Davis
President.

Alfred Paschall
Secretary.

No. 259

Mercer was always interested in the Bucks County Historical Society. He was an early vice president and donated a large building for a museum, together with his unique collection of early American tools. Shown is a membership certificate dated 1899.

The founder and first president of the Bucks County Historical Society was Gen. W.W.H. Davis, to whom this book is dedicated. He is seated at his desk at the society's headquarters, c. 1900.

Elkins Hall was the first permanent building of the Bucks County Historical Society. Before the construction of Elkins Hall, dedicated in 1907, the society had used a room in the 1878 Bucks County Court House.

This wing of the Bucks County Historical Society was given by Henry Mercer to house his collection of early American tools and other artifacts. The wing, built of concrete, is shown under construction.

38

This is another view of the Mercer wing of the Bucks County Historical Society during an early stage of construction. The rear facade of the Elkins Building appears at left.

Finally, the Mercer wing of the Bucks County Historical Society was completed. The Elkins Building is joined to the Mercer wing by an enclosed breezeway. The two buildings are known today as the Mercer Museum.

The front of Elkins Hall is in the foreground, with Mercer's addition to the rear.

The amphitheater of the Mercer Museum contains some of Mercer's collection of tools and machinery, which are attached to and suspended from almost every available surface.

Individual display rooms are located around the central vaulted area, or amphitheater, of the Mercer Museum. This one contains a carpenter's sliding-catch bench and associated items. Many appeared in eastern Pennsylvania in the mid-to-late 19th century.

This is the Spruance Library before remodeling. It contains an outstanding collection of books, prints, maps, and manuscripts related to Bucks County and is part of the Bucks County Historical Society.

An old log cabin, c. 1750, stood on the grounds of the Mercer Museum. The cabin burned several years ago and was replaced with a copy of the original.

In 1928, Henry Mercer's brother, William Mercer, tore down the family's residence, Aldie, on the outskirts of the borough and erected an expansive manor house, which still stands. The razing of the homestead led to family friction, which was unresolved at Henry's death in 1930. Shown is the new Aldie behind the fence and wall. It is now the headquarters of the Heritage Conservancy, a nonprofit organization that preserves land and buildings in Bucks County.

Four

THE MILITARY

Doylestown participated only to a limited extent in the American Revolution and the War of 1812, but it played a significant role in the Civil War, largely because of one resident—W.W.H. Davis. Born in nearby Davisville on July 27, 1820, he attended a private school in Doylestown and studied law at Harvard. Davis, whose father was a general during the American Revolution, was a lieutenant in the Mexican War and was promoted to captain. In 1853, he was appointed U.S. attorney by President Franklin Pierce for the then-territory of New Mexico and later became its attorney general. He authored *El Gringo: New Mexico and Her People* (Harper and Brothers, 1857) and altogether wrote ten books. Upon his return in 1857, he bought a newspaper, the *Doylestown Democrat*, and also practiced law. He lived on East Court Street across from the Bucks County Court House. He twice ran for Congress, unsuccessfully. He died in 1910 and is buried in Doylestown Cemetery.

In the war years of the 1860s, Doylestown—and Davis—played an important part. At the outset of the Civil War, he recruited "the Doylestown Guards," a volunteer unit. After its disbanding, Davis organized a regiment of infantry, the famous 104th Pennsylvania Volunteers, and became its colonel. He and his men fought with distinction at the Battle of Fair Oaks, at Charleston. Discharged in 1864, the regiment was given a welcoming reception at the Bucks County Court House in Doylestown. Davis was breveted a brigadier general in 1865 for his outstanding service. In 1868, under his direction, a monument was erected that stands at the top of the Main Street hill.

Many Doylestonians have participated in the wars and military actions that followed Davis's time, and the borough has a number of military monuments and veterans' organizations. On May 12, 1894, Sgt. Hiram W. Pursell, a member of the 104th Pennsylvania Volunteers, was awarded the Congressional Medal of Honor for valor during the Civil War. He is believed to be the only recipient of that great honor to have come from Doylestown.

Lt. Harry Kessler of the 104th Regiment of Pennsylvania Volunteers sits for his photograph in Philadelphia. The commanding officer of this Doylestown-based regiment was Col. W.W.H. Davis (later a general). In his book *Doylestown, Old and New*, published in 1904, Davis wrote extensively about the battles in which the regiment engaged and its movements as far south as South Carolina. It also had garrison duty in Florida.

Officers and men of the 104th Pennsylvania Volunteers attend a reunion and stand on the steps of the 1878 Bucks County Court House. Each person at the reunion received a gift from John Wanamaker.

After the Civil War, Harry Kessler left the Doylestown area and became a frontier military commander. He is seated at a typical campaign desk of the period.

A band plays at the Civil War Monument in Monument Square, Doylestown, at one of the 104th Regiment's reunions, c. 1909. Davis had tried, unsuccessfully, to have the monument erected in the Doylestown Cemetery. Long after his retirement from the army, he remained active in the regiment's activities and was the main speaker at its 40th reunion in 1901, when

he was 81 years old. Doylestown has paid homage to its veterans of each of the wars and military actions of the 20th century and has dedicated several monuments that are located in the courthouse park. In this picture, the band members are from the Boys' Brigade of Doylestown, and the veterans are beribboned and wearing white gloves.

The Soldiers' Memorial honors the men of Doylestown who served in World War I. It originally stood in the park that adjoined the second Bucks County Court House, but is now behind the present courthouse, near the corner of Main and Broad Streets. The sculptor was William Mercer-Henry's brother, and the models were Russell Gulick and Raymond Rutherford.

Soldiers are marching at the 1938 Centennial Celebration in Doylestown, honoring the incorporation of the borough.

The armory of the National Guard is located on Shewell Avenue and is still in use. For many years, it was used for high school basketball games and other activities.

HONOR ROLL, DOYLESTOWN, PA.

HONOR ROLL

This honor roll listed the men and women from Doylestown who served in the armed forces in Word War II. In the late 1940s, it mysteriously disappeared and has never been found.

This building from the turn of the 19th century once housed the Veterans of Foreign Wars post. Still standing, it is located diagonally across from Doylestown's railroad station.

Many of the veterans' organizations sponsor social and civic events, as well as military ceremonies. Here is an Easter egg hunt at American Legion Post No. 210 in 1983.

Five

TRANSPORTATION AND COMMUNICATION

Doylestown, like many small towns, was quite isolated until the middle of the 19th century. Then, as a result of changes in transportation and communication throughout America around 1850, the borough became more closely linked with other American towns and cities.

In 1845–1846, the telegraph came to the borough, connecting New York and Norristown via Doylestown. It was the first section of a large line running between New York and Washington. The stagecoach still existed, but by the fall of 1856, the first train had already stopped in Doylestown. Also, national fads and enthusiasms were creeping in. The historian W.W.H. Davis reported in his 1904 book *Doylestown, Old and New* that when he lived at the Fountain House, the famous local hotel, in the 1850s, "'table turning,' a necromancy with which electricity and galvanism had to do, made its appearance here." In 1898, the first trolley car appeared, with tracks having been laid along Main Street, making it possible to ride to Willow Grove to the south and to Trenton, New Jersey, about 30 miles away.

A buckboard and delivery wagon are shown in front of Heist's Hotel, 1882. The hotel was later known as the Court Inn.

The stagecoach arrives outside the Fountain House. This moment is probably from Doylestown's Old Home Week of 1912, celebrating the 100th anniversary of the opening of the first Bucks County Court House.

A delivery wagon for the Pell Company is parked on West State Street, next to the Doylestown Inn, 1912. Note the banner advertising the Walsh Decorating Company.

The Doylestown railroad station, c. 1907, still exists. It was the end of the line on a Reading Railroad route and is now a Southeastern Pennsylvania Transportation Authority (SEPTA) station.

Telephone cables are being laid near the corner of West Court and State Streets, 1905. The building—much modified—remains and is now a fine Italian restaurant.

The Bell Telephone Company had its office on Main Street around the turn of the 19th century. The building was next-door to the former Hart Bank.

A trolley car nears the central span on the Tohicken Creek Bridge near Doylestown.

A car of the Willow Grove Trolley Company, 1900, is seen with a corner of the balcony of the Fountain House in the background.

In this early-1900s photograph, a car belonging to what was then the Philadelphia Rapid Transit Company is stopped in downtown Doylestown.

The tracks of the Willow Grove Trolley Company were installed shortly before the turn of the 19th century. The whole town was excited by the arrival of the first trolley car in May 1898.

An early automobile is driven in the Doylestown area, *c.* 1910.

Shown in 1915, this motorized delivery truck was owned by the Henry S. Beisler Company.

This delivery truck was owned by William Neis's Whistle Bottling Company, makers of Whistle, an orange soda.

A chemical engine, or fire truck, is shown outside Doylestown's firehouse, which exists and is in use.

This building contained Doylestown's post office. It was built by the Works Progress Administration c. 1936 with no off-street parking. The photograph was probably taken in the 1940s. The building survives and is now occupied by an engineering firm. A new post office, with a large parking area, was constructed on Atkinson Lane.

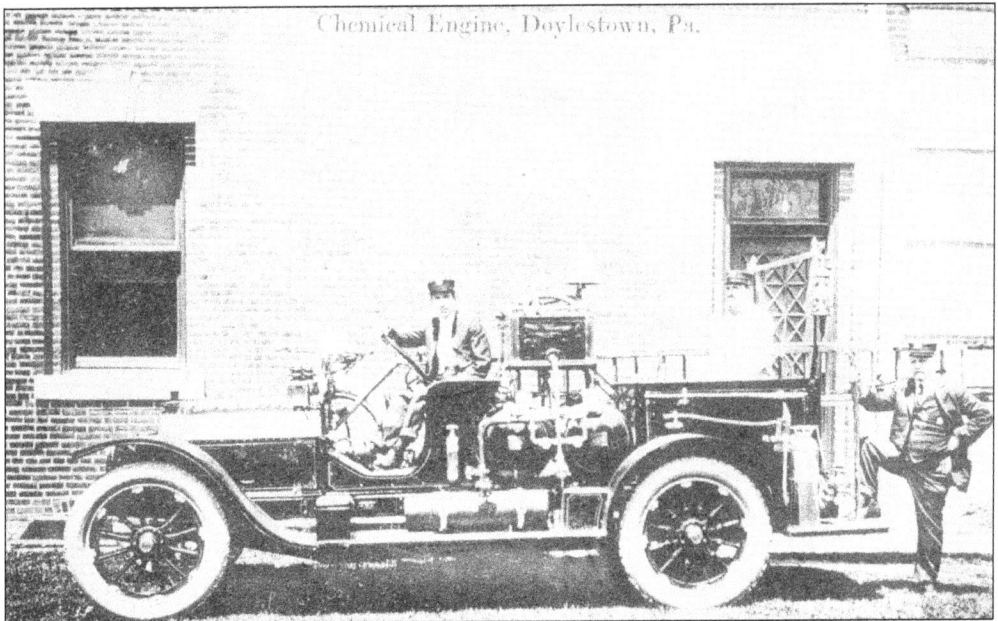

The Doylestown Volunteer Fire Company building has just been constructed. Old firefighting equipment is shown in front of the structure.

Doylestown citizens proudly pose in an early 1900s automobile. This photograph was taken during Old Home Week in 1912.

Harrison-Yerkes advertises its livery stable on York (now Oakland Avenue) Street: "Passengers met at Rail-Road-Depot and conveyed to all parts of the county."

Six

STREETS AND ROADS

Doylestown has been noted for its historic buildings for many years. It contains fine Pennsylvania Dutch fieldstone houses and Victorian brick houses. After the Civil War, there was a flurry of building, but the early 20th century was not particularly kind to the borough. Old buildings fell into disrepair and a few were razed; much of Main Street was boarded up or struggled for survival. The irony was that Doylestown's comparative isolation in the early 20th century meant that many of its structures were not torn down. By the late 1920s and early 1930s, the old buildings—and especially the unique structures designed and built by Henry Mercer, as well as his extraordinary collection of artifacts—began to attract tourists and other visitors. Today, Doylestown is well known for many kinds of historic structures as well as its wealth of handsome gardens and its labyrinth of charming alleyways.

A bird's-eye view of Doylestown is shown in an early 1900s postcard.

Easton Road, later part of U.S. Route 611, ran from Doylestown to Willow Grove to the south and Easton to the north. Note the tracks for the Willow Grove trolley beside the road.

This is the center of the downtown, Main and State Streets (1909). The Fountain House is at the right. Across State Street is the former Mansion House building. Through the years, this intersection has dominated the life and business of the borough.

This is Main Street, looking south, about a half a block below the courthouse and Monument Square. The former Hart Bank building, which survives, in the left foreground.

Near the same corner, years later, a car on the left is stopped on State Street for the traffic signal. The Lenape Building is at the left rear, and the Fountain House Hotel is on the right.

This is North Main Street, across from the courthouse. The house on the left, formerly a funeral home, is now used by First Service Bank for its administrative offices.

Here, at the intersection of West Court Street and State Street, the house at the corner still exists, but is now a restaurant.

On South Main Street, the former home of the Methodist Church is on the right (1909). The trolley line left Doylestown many years ago, and the tracks were eventually removed. As one enters Doylestown from the south, there is a long hill leading to Monument Square and

the courthouse. Starting in the foreground of this picture, there are four successive blocks with traffic signals. Despite the construction of the Doylestown bypass some years ago, traffic congestion has become an increasing problem, particularly on Main Street.

On West State Street, near Main, Kenny's News and Rutherford's Camera Shop, two local landmarks, appear at left.

On State Street, probably in the 1920s, the Lenape Building stands in the background at left rear.

On Court Street, not far from the former courthouse, the Intelligencer building is at the right. Note the community water fountain. Many of the old houses survive and have been made into law offices. On East Court Street, the buildings are called "Lawyers' Row." The Intelligencer, Doylestown's daily newspaper, moved its operations in the 1970s to new and much larger quarters on Broad Street.

Farther out East Court Street, near Spruce Street, on the way to Henry Mercer's Fonthill, the spire of the Presbyterian Church rises in the background.

At the corner of Court Street and Broad Street, the building at right was once a bank and later a public library. It now is occupied by the county controller's office.

Oakland Avenue is primarily a residential street, but is also the location of St. Paul's Episcopal Church and the Friends Meeting. Doylestown's first hospital was here, at the corner of Church Street.

Ashland Street, near Main, is the site of large, turn-of-the-century houses and the Mercer Museum.

Pine Run Creek, near Doylestown, is a tributary of Neshaminy Creek and a part of the county's water conservation program.

This large house on East Court Street was built for a prominent local resident, Caroline Shellenberger. It was later used as a home for deaf mutes. Today it is occupied by Doylestown's Conservatory of Music and also by its owner, the Salem United Church of Christ, the church building for which is located across the street.

The parsonage of the former Baptist Church is now the Landmark Building. The parsonage has been remodeled and is now connected to the former church.

A portion of the Dubois House, Doylestown, was converted to a shop. The main part of the house was demolished.

The Senator Grim House (later the Kenny House) is at the corner of Main and Broad Streets. It is now the office of the law firm of Dommel and Hill.

The Enoch Harvey house, on Main Street, was torn down at the turn of the century to make room for the Hart Building.

The Beatty House is located at the corner of State and Broad Streets. Before the Civil War, it was one of Doylestown's stations on the Underground Railroad, which aided slaves to escape to Canada. It is one block from the courthouse and is now law offices.

This Doylestown residence at East State and Broad Streets was formerly owned by attorney Howard Barnes, who was executive vice president of the Doylestown National Bank for many years in the mid-1900s.

The Shoemaker House on Court Street at West Street in Doylestown is known today as the Margaret Mead House. The famous anthropologist lived here as a teenager and graduated from Doylestown High School.

The Thomas Ross Residence in Doylestown was formerly the Indian Queen Inn (1811). The house was demolished in 1896.

The Chestnut Grove Mansion, later a hotel, is an example of the large estates that were once built near Doylestown.

Seven

PRIVATE AND PUBLIC LIFE IN DOYLESTOWN

Among the people who lived in Doylestown were both the obscure and the famous—people who were not known outside the borough but also famous Americans, such as Oscar Hammerstein II, who had chosen Doylestown for its beauty, the "civilized" quality of central Bucks County, and its proximity to the major cities of the Middle Atlantic region. This chapter contains photographic moments in the lives of a few residents of Doylestown, as well as poses of some of the celebrities who selected the Doylestown area, often as a weekend home, who came from New York and Philadelphia and other cities and who frequented the borough.

A Doylestown woman is shown in the early 1900s.

A youthful Frank P. Kolbe is contemplating a long ride on his bicycle, probably in the early 1900s. "Frisco or Bust" is the legend on this photograph.

A man stands for his photograph at the Craven Studio, probably in the 1890s. Craven was a well-known Doylestown photographer whose postcard reproductions are voluminous.

This photograph was also taken in the Craven Studio in the late 1800s. African American families trace their roots in Doylestown to the 18th century. According to Wilma Rezer, a local historian, two former slaves, Cudjo and Jo, were bequeathed land on East Court Street in the mid-1700s by the man who emancipated them.

Baseball became popular in Doylestown soon after it was introduced by Abner Doubleday. Here, a game is played on the Doylestown Grounds with the Doylestown team seated in front of the stands on June 8, 1889. In those days, Doylestown played teams from a number of colleges.

Since then, Little League, girls' softball, and teenage and adult baseball have become part of the life of the area. (From Spruance Library, Bucks County Historical Society.)

George P. Brock's Brass Orchestra was a group of amateurs who played at open-air concerts in the courthouse park in the summers of 1887 through 1890. This photograph was taken on August 1, 1888. (From Spruance Library, Bucks County Historical Society.)

The Boys' Brigade, founded by George Murray in 1907, was a forerunner of the Boy Scouts. Many of Doylestown's young men were members, including Jim Michener. Murray devoted himself for 25 years to "his boys," who drilled in uniform, played basketball, had a band, and went to summer camp—at no cost to them. The Boys' Brigade was a Doylestown institution. (From Spruance Library, Bucks County Historical Society.)

Doylestown's first and perhaps only grass tennis court was constructed on Oakland Avenue. The men are wearing trousers, and a woman is playing in a long dress.

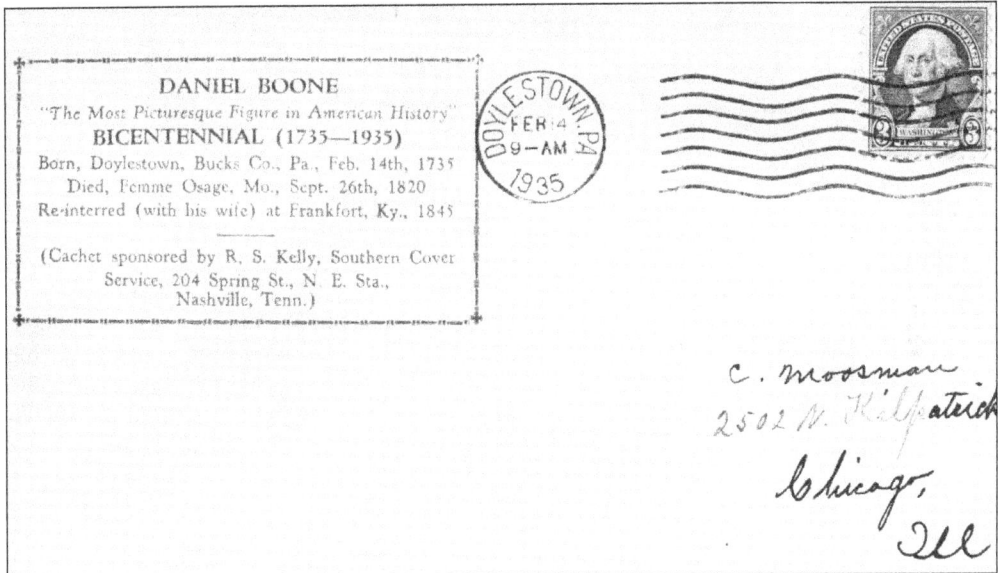

This bicentennial cover, postmarked February 14, 1935, celebrates the birth of Daniel Boone in Doylestown on that date in 1735. Boone's parents lived in Bucks County for a time, but historians today believe that he was born in 1734 in Birdsboro, Pennsylvania, near Reading in Berks County.

A
Well-Known Doylestown
Citizen

Shown is a portrait of William Neis, a leading business and political figure in the late 19th and early 20th century. His son, also William Neis, is now the mayor of Doylestown Borough. In 1904, the elder William Neis bought out a wholesale liquor and bottling business, having operated the Railroad House, an inn, for 16 years. His business became the supplier of more than 60 hotels in Bucks County. He also was a member of the Doylestown Borough Council.

Among the most celebrated of Doylestown's residents was Oscar Hammerstein II (1895–1960), the Broadway lyricist and librettist who worked with some of the outstanding names in American theatre, including Lorenz Hart and Richard Rodgers. Hammerstein wrote the libretto for *South Pacific* (1949) after the book by James Michener. (From the James A. Michener Art Museum.)

George Kaufman (1889–1961) and
Moss Hart (1904–1961), two famous
Broadway playwrights and good friends,
had homes in the Doylestown area,
Kaufman on Route 202 and Hart
on nearby Aquetong Road. The two
men wrote several hugely successful
plays together, among them *Once in a
Lifetime*, *You Can't Take It with You*,
and *The Man Who Came to Dinner*.
(From the James A. Michener
Art Museum.)

Pearl Buck (1892–1973), the novelist,
owned a farm near Doylestown. It is
now owned by a foundation bearing
her name and is open to the public.
(From the James A. Michener
Art Museum.)

James Michener (1907–1997) grew up in Doylestown a poor boy, without knowing Hammerstein, who was to base perhaps his most famous adaptation for the stage on two stories from the Pulitzer Prize–winning book *South Pacific*. After their theatrical success, Michener purchased a farm near Doylestown. In 1964, he unsuccessfully ran for Congress. He wrote 48 books and gave away more than $100 million. (From the James A. Michener Art Museum.)

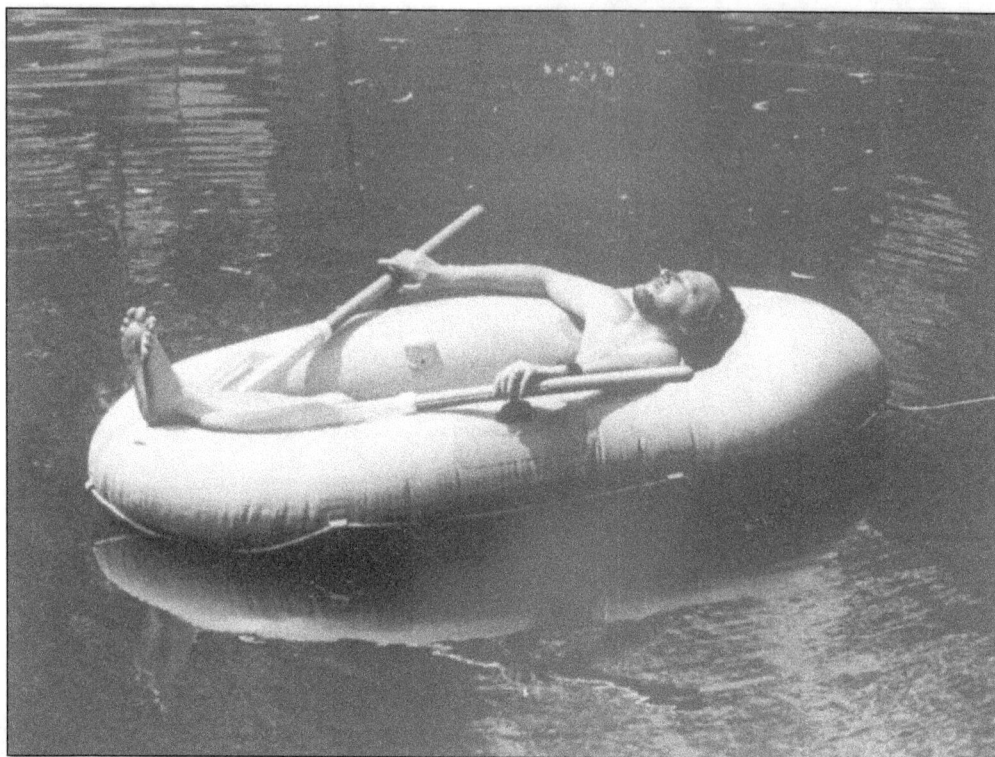

Stephen Sondheim spent his high school years here and attended nearby George School. His mother owned a farm near Doylestown. The young Sondheim was friendly with the Hammerstein family and got his start in show business from Oscar Hammerstein II. (From the James A. Michener Art Museum.)

Writer S.J. Perelman (1904–1979), many of whose humorous pieces appeared in the *New Yorker* magazine, had a farm near Doylestown and often wrote about his experiences in rural Bucks County. (From the James A. Michener Art Museum.)

Eight

CELEBRATIONS

The people of Doylestown have always been interested in community celebrations. One took place in 1865 at the news of Sherman's victory over Lee. Another was staged in 1878, marking 100 years since the first recorded reference to "Doylestown" as a single word. Flags flew over the borough, and on the morning of March 1, 1878, there was a procession through the streets, portraying the trades and occupations of the area. The printing offices were represented by a press and the blacksmiths by a wagon on which a horse was being shoed. The procession also contained representatives of the borough's beneficial societies, the Boys of America, the Doylestown Hose Company, and many citizens of the borough. The celebration of the bicentennial of Bucks County was held here in 1882. Over the years, other celebrations included one on Armistice Day 1918, and the so-called Great War Veterans' Parade of 1919. Two that were widely photographed were the 1912 Old Home Week—marking the centennial of the dedication of the first courthouse in Doylestown after the Pennsylvania legislature had authorized the removal of the county seat from Newtown—and the 1938 Doylestown Borough centennial marking the incorporation of the borough. In 1988, Doylestown celebrated the sesquicentennial of its incorporation with great fanfare and activity, much of which is commemorated in a large pictorial book, *Doylestown 150 Years*.

Marchers parade in 18th-century dress at the 1912 Old Home Week.

A float passes by in the 1912 parade, sponsored by a local organization.

Firemen are marching on Main Street during Old Home Week in 1912. They are moving up the hill toward the courthouse, having passed the Hart Building, which appears in the background.

A float of the Washington Camp of the Patriotic Sons of America participated in the 1912 Old Home Week.

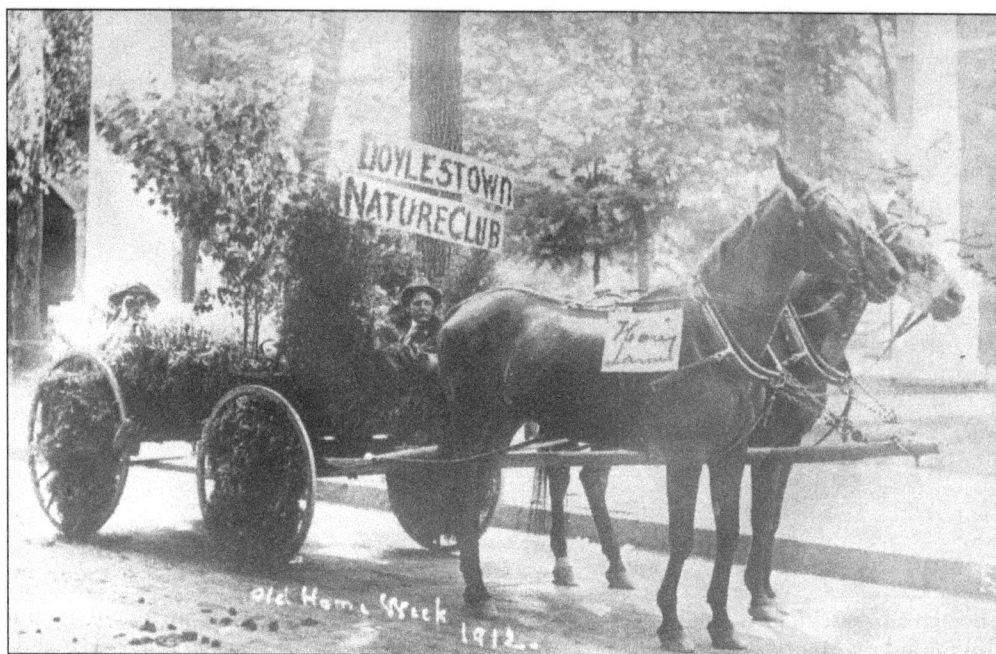

The Doylestown Nature Club had its headquarters in one of the buildings at Fonthill. Here is its float in the 1912 Old Home Week parade.

A part of the Old Home Week parade featured a horse-drawn float. Straw hats and large bonnets abound, and every building is festooned with the Stars and Stripes. (From Spruance Library, Bucks County Historical Society.)

There was a Court of Honor, probably on East Court Street, 1912.

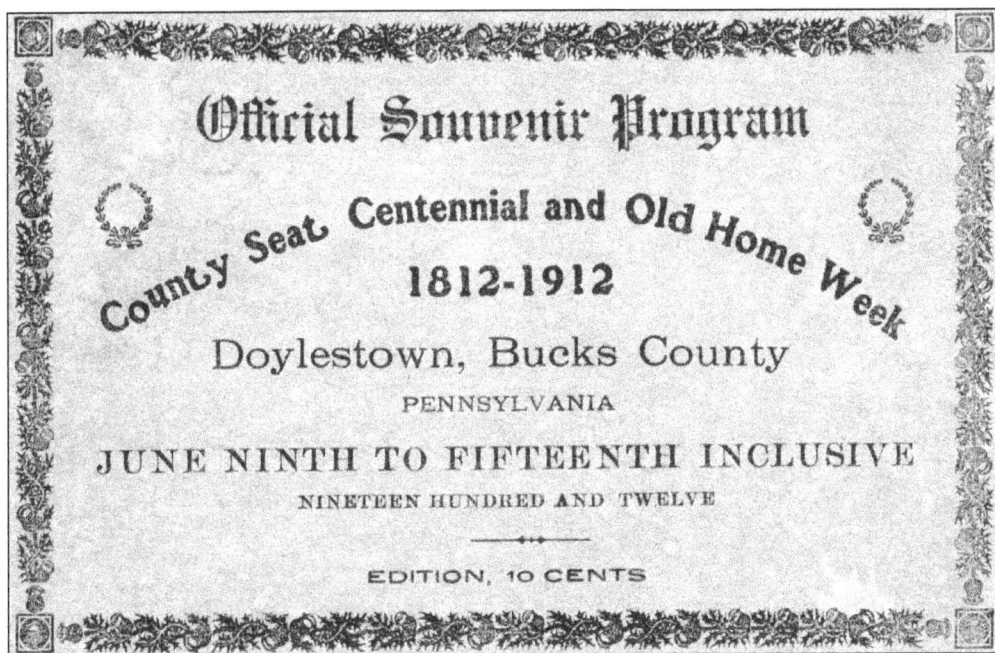

Official Souvenir Program

County Seat Centennial and Old Home Week

1812-1912

Doylestown, Bucks County

PENNSYLVANIA

JUNE NINTH TO FIFTEENTH INCLUSIVE

NINETEEN HUNDRED AND TWELVE

EDITION, 10 CENTS

This souvenir program was published for Old Home Week in 1912, "June ninth to fifteenth inclusive."

Alfresco dancing occurs in 18th-century costume during Old Home Week in 1912. This courtly scene before an appreciative audience probably took place on a street in the downtown. It reflects the considerable enthusiasm of the local citizenry for participating in community

celebrations. There continue to be large-scale dances held in and near Doylestown, sometimes at the Mercer estate (Aldie), at Fonthill, or at the Bucks County Bar Association building. Costume balls, however, are not as popular as they used to be.

A float goes by in the 1938 parade, celebrating the borough's incorporation in 1838. Much time and effort went into producing this elaborate float, advertising Scheetz's "Ladies Ready to Wear Shop," and the costumes for the young women who adorn it. At right, spectators young and old observe the bedecked float as it passes the Doylestown National Bank on East Court Street near Monument Square. The whole town has turned out for the parade.

For the 1938 parade, this wagon was converted to a float by Histand Brothers, a roofing company that still exists, passed down from one generation to the next. Parades in Doylestown have been a community tradition, although there may be fewer nowadays than there used to be. The ever popular Memorial Day parade draws large crowds along Main, State, and Court Streets; in recent years, on Food, Fun, and Fitness Day (held on the same weekend), the streets have been closed, and more than 10,000 people have congregated in the center of the borough.

A "wooden nickel" was made for the 1938 celebration.

In the 1938 Centennial Celebration, a band is marching down what is probably West Court Street. The 1938 celebration was in honor of the incorporation of the borough in 1838. The 1912 Centennial Celebration honored the dedication of the first Bucks County Court House.

Program

•

Doylestown Centennial

In Commemoration of the 100th Anniversary of the Incorporation of Doylestown as a Borough

•

May 29 to June 4, 1938

(All times given are Daylight Saving)

A program cover from the 1938 celebration marks the week-long festivities, from May 29 to June 4.

Nine

TOURISM

By the 1830s, what had once been a tiny hamlet had developed into a pleasant, rather cultivated and relatively busy place, with more than 100 houses and the usual merchants, businessmen, and professional people. By the 1840s, the borough was becoming a summer resort, especially for the people of nearby Philadelphia, which accounts for the large number of hotels and inns that existed in and around Doylestown. A local newspaper of the 1840s announced, "We present our annual invitation to our Philadelphia friends to come up and breathe the pure atmosphere of the hill during the summer heat." The lines that W.W.H. Davis wrote on the last page of his turn-of-the-century book are still true today: "The location of Doylestown is an ideal site for a country borough and cannot be excelled . . . . The country around it is picturesque, rich, and health, and, from the steeple of the Court House, the view is charming, equaling anything Midland England presents."

William Doyle, after whom the town is named, opened his tavern in 1745 near the crossroads that became Main and State Streets, the center of the downtown.

Cross Keys Tavern, first licensed in 1758, later became Conti's Cross Keys Inn, a popular restaurant until a few years ago. The original tavern building still exists, but most of the site is now occupied by a service station.

This is an early print of Magill's Mansion House, c. 1805, at State and Main Streets, Doylestown. Originally a residence and later a hotel, the building is now the home of the Paper Unicorn, a stationery and gift shop.

THE MONUMENT HOUSE, DOYLESTOWN, PA.

J. G. MITCHELL, Proprietor

Splendid Menu   Ample Garage Facilities

The Monument House in Doylestown, shown c. 1924, was razed in 1964. It stood on North Main Street and was originally called Heist's Inn and, later, the Court Inn.

An advertising card from the Monument House reads, "The Monument House is good enough for everybody and not too good for anybody."

Doylestown's well-known hotel, the Fountain House, was once the Doylestown Hotel. It is located at the corner of Main and State Streets in the heart of the downtown and is presently used for a coffee shop and offices.

104

The old, picturesque grill room of the Fountain House is shown as it appeared in the mid-20th century, before it was completely remodeled. After the hotel was closed, the building was occupied as a furniture store and then a bank before it was converted to its present use.

The Railroad Hotel (or Railroad House) stood on South Clinton Street across from the railroad station.

The Bucks County Inn is another relic of Doylestown's past tourist industry. The building was demolished, and a bank was built on the site, which is on Main Street across from the courthouse park.

The Oakland House, a resort on West Street, was once a private boys' school. It no longer exists.

The Monument House was refurbished and renamed the Court Inn. Note the arcade at the side of the building.

The Chestnut Grove Mansion in later years became a boardinghouse not far from the center of the downtown.

The Doylestown Inn, on State Street near Main, has been completely renovated. For many years, it was a successful restaurant. In the 1930s, Sunday dinners were so popular that people lined up on the sidewalk waiting for a table. This view of the inn predates World War II.

The lobby of the Doylestown Inn, like the Grill Room at the Fountain House, has been lost in the process of reconstruction.

The Clear Springs Hotel, 1890, was located on North Main Street in an area that was known as "Germany" because a large number of persons of German descent resided there. The hotel was demolished in 1969.

Another view of the Railroad House shows the alteration of the balcony rails and the buggies parked by the hotel.

The States Tourist Cottages, located at the southern end of Doylestown on Route 611, are shown in a 1930s or 1940s postcard. Individual cottages were named after various states.

Kram's Hotel, at Court and Pine Streets, is shown in an old pen and ink drawing. (From Spruance Library, Bucks County Historical Society.)

The former Water Wheel Inn (1714) on Old Easton Road, which became the Pear and Partridge Inn, is now the Sign of the Sorrel House.

Conti's Cross Keys Inn, 1958, Doylestown's best-known restaurant in the latter half of the 20th century, was demolished in the 1990s. Operated by the Conti family since the repeal of Prohibition in 1932, it drew patrons from far and wide for 65 years.

Ed's Diner, on West State Street, was a popular eating place from the 1940s to the 1970s. As the restaurant prospered over the years, Ed would purchase a new and larger diner. This is the last and the most modern-looking building.

The former Water Wheel Inn, shown here in another view, was located a mile and a half north of Doylestown in a pleasant setting.

Ten

INDUSTRY AND COMMERCE

Downtown Doylestown is also filled with fine old commercial buildings, many of which have survived to the present. The Lenape Building, for example, at the corner of Main and State Streets, is still used for shops and offices. Built in 1874, it cost the then-huge sum of $50,000, and more than 800 people attended its dedication. As originally conceived, the building contained five stores, a theatre, two lodge rooms, and a market facility on the south side of the ground floor. The clock on the corner of the building was "a present from a lady of Doylestown," according to Davis's history. The last decades of the 19th century saw the construction of an elaborate office block known as the Hart Building, which still stands on Main Street. In recent years, the Agricultural Works and the Art Deco County Theater have been restored. They are now occupied by a restaurant and offices and a community-sponsored fine films movie house, respectively. A former bank building on Monument Square is being converted into offices and a banquet facility.

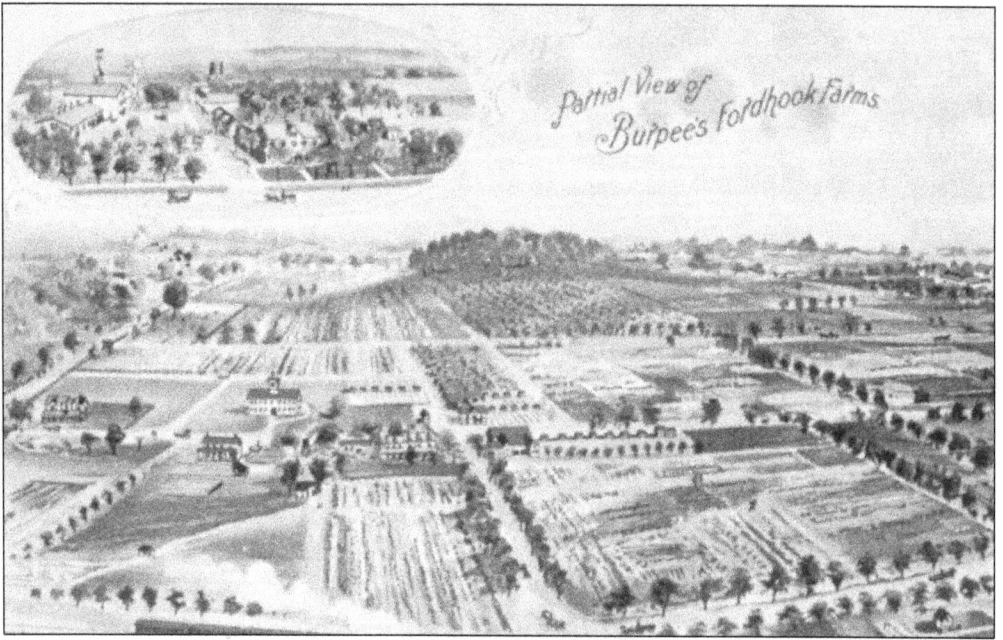

Shown in an aerial view is W. Atlee Burpee's famous Fordhook Farms, near Doylestown. In 1913, Burpee—in honor of his wife, Blanche—gave the borough a square block of land to be used for a children's park.

The trial grounds at Fordhook Farms, W. Atlee Burpee's estate and truck farm, served the needs of the Burpee Seed Company, which prospered and became known internationally.

Lenape Hall, at Main and State Streets, Doylestown, was the borough's main commercial building from the late 1800s into the mid-1900s. The name "Lenape" was derived from the Native American tribe known as "Leni-Lenape" or "Lenni-Lenape," who inhabited the Delaware River Valley. The name is well-preserved in Doylestown not only by this building, but also by the Lenape Junior High School, located on the edge of the borough.

The Agricultural Works, or "Ag Works" (1867) on South Main Street, was where threshers and cutting machines were once made—the chief industry in Doylestown in the 19th century. The building is shown as it was in the 1890s. Remodeled in the 1980s, it is occupied by a restaurant and offices. It was owned for one day in the 1920s by General Motors.

"Ag Works" employees are shown in the 1890s.

116

William Neis's bottling works were located in a building that still exists on East State Street.

Shive's hardware store was a downtown landmark, situated at the corner of Main and State Streets across from the Lenape Building and the Fountain House. An upscale carpet store is now at the site.

The Fisher blacksmith shop building on State Street (shown) became Kenny's News in the 1940s. Part of the structure that contains the Rutherford Camera Shop is visible on the left. Both were part of the so-called Foulke Purchase.

The Hart Building, shown c. 1896 on Main Street, was described by W.W.H. Davis in his book on Doylestown as one of the most beautiful buildings in Pennsylvania.

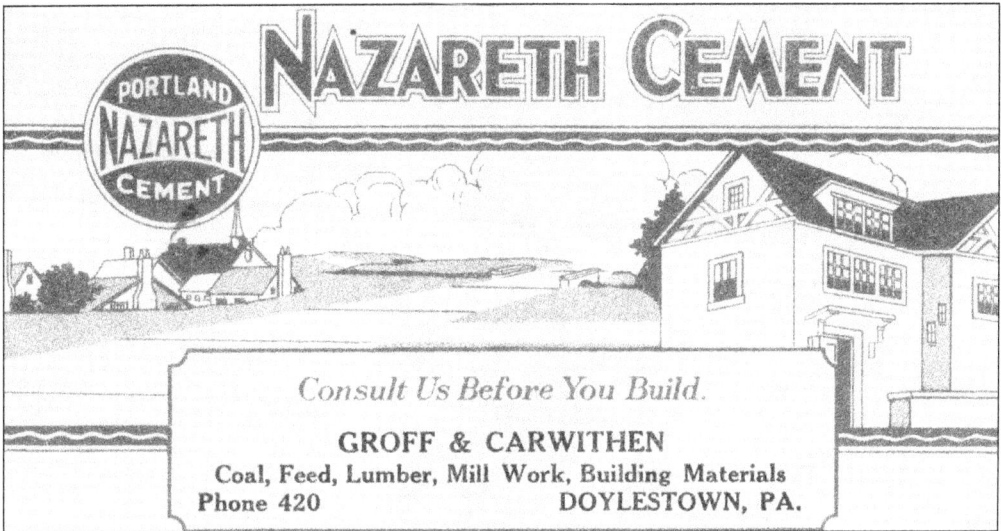

An advertisement for Groff and Carwithen lists coal, lumber, millwork, and other building materials and features Nazareth Cement.

Ely's grocery store was located on South Main Street, c. 1920.

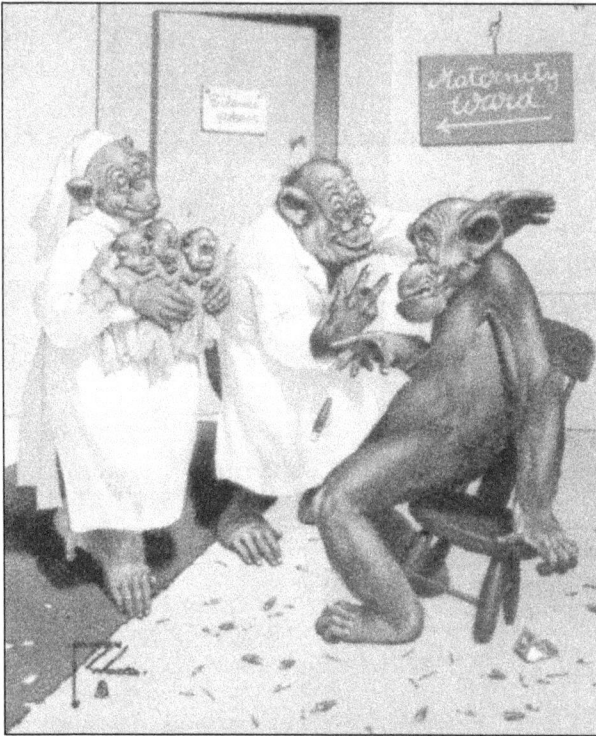

This advertisement was for Ben's Auto Body Shop at Cross Keys, at the northern end of the borough. It is still operated by Ben and his family. "Chimp" humor was popular in advertisements and other items of the 1930s and 1940s.

One could relax at the bar of the Doylestown Inn on State Street near Main in the early 1900s. After the 1940s, while it continued to be a local landmark, the inn went through a succession of owners. Closed for the past two years, it is undergoing extensive renovations.

120

Michael A. Rufe, a plumber and dealer in plumbing supplies, had his shop on Taylor Alley, between Main and Pine Streets.

Workers stand outside the Fisher Cigar Factory in the 1870s. The building is now part of the Doylestown Inn.

The Woman with an All-Gas Kitchen

She cooks *best*, in the *least* time; has the *most* time for rest and recreation, *never* has to handle a dirty, dusty ash pan, nor a heavy shovel or coal bucket.

Her kitchen is the *cleanest* and *handiest* and the cooking is the *most economical* because GAS is the *cheapest* kitchen fuel.

Hot Water as you wish it. One gallon per foot of Gas consumed.

A Card from you and our demonstrator will call and explain

The Doylestown Gas Co.

Show Room, Randall's Store, at Main and State Streets

This advertisement for the Doylestown Gas Company lists a showroom in Randall's Store at Main and State Streets, probably in the early 1900s.

Clymer's Store was located at Clinton and Ashland Streets. Later, this general store was relocated to Main Street between State Street and Oakland Avenue and became the largest department store in the area.

Harvey's Drug Store on Main Street, 1896, was torn down for the Hart Building. Until the latter part of the 19th century, there were a number of drugstores and apothecary shops in Doylestown. The drugstores usually had soda fountains. With the coming of supermarkets, shopping centers, and soda dispensing machines, drugstores and small grocery stores disappeared.

Ely's Men's Store at Main and Court Streets advertises Michael Stern Clothes. In the mid-1900s, this was the leading men's clothing store in Doylestown.

Scheetz's Department Store, 1912, is decked out for Old Home Week, one of the biggest celebrations ever held in Doylestown.

124

According to this advertisement for Dr. Hayman's private hospital, East State Street, one could obtain "Examination Without Charge or Obligation." The site is now occupied by the Bucks County Bar Association's headquarters.

On November 1, 1921, President Judge William C. Ryan of the Bucks County Court of Common Pleas was billed $5 for storing his car for a month by Atkinson's Garage on Oakland Avenue, "Bell Phone Garage 267, Residence 297."

A $20 bill, series 1929, contains the imprint of the Doylestown National Bank and Trust Company. In the days on the brink of the Great Depression, National Banks could still issue paper money.

The Bucks County Trust Company was located on Court Street at Monument Square. The structure became the Doylestown National Bank and Trust Company.

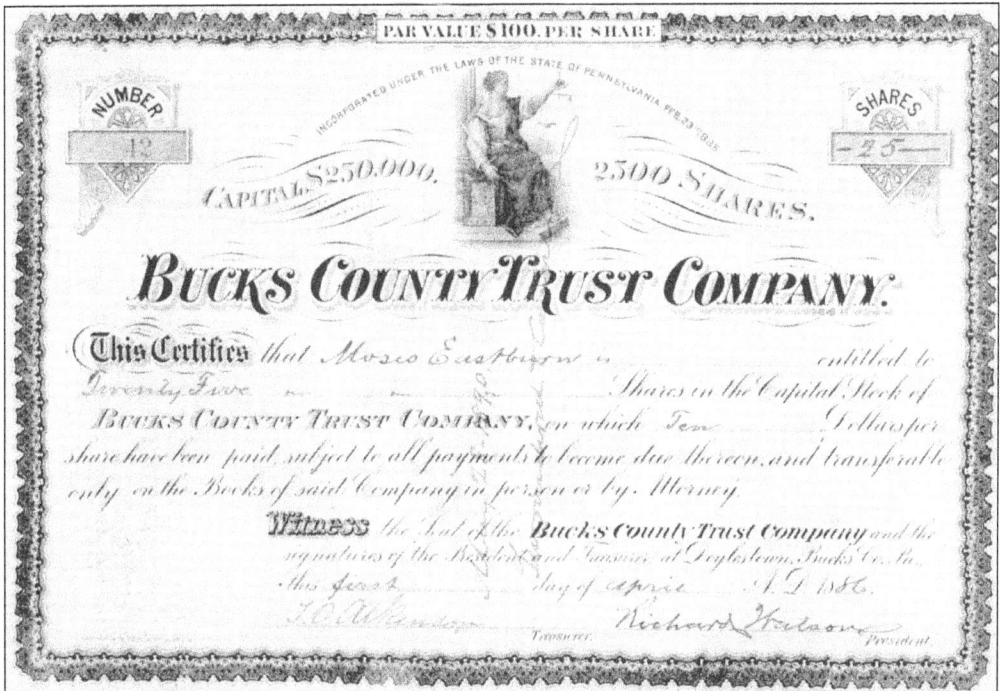

This stock certificate for 25 shares of the Bucks County Bank and Trust Company at $10 per share was issued to Moses Eastburn on April 1, 1886.

In the editorial room of the Daily Republican newspaper office in Doylestown, five nattily dressed journalists are at work, several of them at typewriters.

END NOTE

In 1992, the Doylestown Borough Council created a task force led by one of its members, Betty Strecker, to study the town's economic and cultural future. In 1993, the council established the Revitalization Board, which elected Ed Ludwig as its first cochair. He served for three years. The Doylestown Historical Society, founded by Ludwig, was an offshoot of the Revitalization Board and continues to be a part of Doylestown Borough. The society's mission is to preserve and commemorate Doylestown's history, an endeavor that is important to the life and welfare of the town. Among a number of projects, the society publishes a biannual newsletter, the *Doylestown Correspondent*, named after one of the town's earliest newspapers. Its editor is Brooks McNamara.

McNamara, Ludwig, and Strecker, respectively, are the author, editor, and coordinator of this book, which the Doylestown Historical Society takes great pride in presenting and hopes you will have enjoyed.

Doylestown Historical Society, Borough Hall, 57 West State Street, Doylestown, Pennsylvania, 18901-4338. Telephone: (215) 345-4140. Fax: (215) 345-8351. E-mail: Admin@DoylestownBorough.net. Website: www.DoylestownBorough.net.

www.ingramcontent.com/pod-product-compliance
Lightning Source LLC
Chambersburg PA
CBHW080855100426
42812CB00007B/2034